Let  Again

Introduction

by Isobel Raine

This book is for the woman who stayed silent
until her voice returned.

For the woman who gave too much
and is learning how to keep something for herself.

For the one who still cries sometimes
but does not break like she used to.

These poems are not about revenge.
They are not about regret.
They are about remembering who you were
before they asked you to be less.

You are not too much.
You are not impossible.
You are not broken.

You are rising.
And you are allowed to do it your way.

Welcome back to yourself.
Welcome back to the wild.

Poem 1: Let Me Be Wild Again

I have been careful
for too long.

Measured my voice,
folded myself in half,
waited to be chosen.

I am done being small.
I was not made to be safe.
Let me be wild again.
Let me be mine.

Poem 2: You Left Quietly

You didn't yell.
You didn't lie.
You just disappeared.

And somehow,
that still bruised more
than all the screaming ever could.

Poem 3: I Took the Long Way Back

I didn't just wake up healed.
I crawled.
I doubted.
I begged myself to try again.

Some mornings, I didn't.
But eventually,
I came home
to the woman I had buried.

Poem 4: I Didn't Ask for Much

I asked for presence.
Not perfection.

For honesty.
Not gifts.

I asked to be seen.
And you blinked
like I was too bright.

Poem 5: The Mirror Doesn't Lie

She looks different now.
Softer.
Tired, but strong.

Not the same girl
who waited for someone
to make her feel
worth loving.

Poem 6: No is a Full Sentence

I used to explain everything.
Why I couldn't come.
Why I changed my mind.
Why I said no.

Now I say it once.
And I say it clear.
No.
Because that is enough.

Poem 7: I Am Not Bitter

I just finally see it.
I see what love is not.
What silence really means.
What it costs to keep trying
when someone has already let go.

That isn't bitterness.
That is clarity.

Poem 8: This Time, I Choose Me

Not out of anger.
Not out of fear.

But because I've learned
what happens
when I don't.
And I won't do that again.

Poem 9: I Am Still Soft

Even after him.
Even after the goodbye
with no reason.

Even after
I had to heal
in silence.

I am still soft.
And that is my strength.

Poem 10: The Fire Stayed Lit

He thought I needed him
to feel warm.

But the fire was always mine.
It just flickered smaller
when I forgot
who I was.

Poem 11: I Remember Her Now

She didn't want much.
Just to feel safe
in the arms she trusted.

Now I look at her differently.
Not as weak.
But as someone who loved
without a backup plan.

Poem 12: I Am Still Learning

Still learning
how to rest.
How to stay.
How to stop asking
if I am too much.

Still learning
that I do not have to earn
every breath of peace.

Poem 13: I'm Not Tired of Loving

I'm just tired
of offering it
to people who leave it
at the door.

Poem 14: The Friend I Needed

She didn't tell me to forget.
She just sat with me
while I remembered.

And I realised
that healing sometimes
sounds like
"I get it."
Not "move on."

Poem 15: I Am Not Who You Left

You left a version of me
that I barely recognise now.

She waited.
She wondered.
She hurt quietly.

This version
doesn't wait.
She walks.

Poem 16: No One Else Decides That

Not my mother.
Not the man who said
he loved me.
Not the silence
I stayed too long in.

No one else decides
who I get to become.

Poem 17: Her Voice Is Back

Not louder.
Not sharper.
Just real.

When she speaks now
she doesn't ask for space.
She claims it.

Poem 18: This Time I Stayed

Not for him.
Not for the old promise.

I stayed for me.
And that changed
everything.

Poem 19: She Grew Around the Wound

It didn't vanish.
It still stings
when she turns too fast.

But she grew around it.
And the blooming
never stopped.

Poem 20: I Am Becoming My Own Shelter

No more waiting
to be saved.

I built a home
from the things I was told
were not enough.

And now
I open the door
only to people
who bring peace inside.

Poem 21: I Was Never Asking Too Much

I just asked
for honesty.
For kindness.
For someone
who would meet me
where I stood.

That was not too much.
They were simply not enough.

Poem 22: Some Days Are Still Heavy

I don't have to smile through all of it.
Some days
I sit in the quiet
and let it ache.

That is not weakness.
That is making room
for truth.

Poem 23: I Am Not the One Who Failed

I gave truth.
I gave time.
I gave everything I had
and still had love left over.

That is not failure.
That is proof.

Poem 24: My Own Peace

I stopped texting first.
I stopped apologising for needing rest.
I stopped explaining the way my heart works.

And the quiet that followed
was the calm
I had been searching for.

Poem 25: The Kind of Woman I Am

I feel everything.
I carry too much.
I hope longer than I should.

But I walk away
when I know I must.
And that part
is always the hardest.

Poem 26: I Have Loved Well

Even when it broke me.
Even when it went unnoticed.

My love has always been
honest.
Messy.
Real.

And that is something
to be proud of.

Poem 27: She Needed Time

Not advice.
Not distraction.

She just needed
time to fall apart
without being asked
to hurry.

Poem 28: I Don't Belong to Anyone

I am not someone's second chance.
I am not waiting
to be chosen.

I belong to myself
and that is more than enough.

Poem 29: I Forgive Myself First

For staying.
For believing.
For all the ways
I gave when I had nothing left.

I forgive the girl
who only wanted
to feel loved.

Poem 30: I Grew in the Dark

No one watered me.
No one checked in.
No one held the light.

But I grew anyway
because I refused
to stay buried.

Poem 31: I Had to Break My Own Pattern

Not just leave him
but leave the part of me
that stayed.

I had to stop confusing
suffering
with love.

Poem 32: She Waited Too Long

She waited for a sign.
For an apology.
For something to tell her
she mattered.

But no one came.
So she stood up
and chose herself.

Poem 33: Not Everyone Will Understand

That's alright.
Let them call it cold.
Let them think you changed too much.

You're not here
to explain your healing
to anyone.

Poem 34: I Did Not Deserve That

No matter how kind I was.
How much I loved.
How quiet I stayed.

None of it meant
I deserved the way
they treated me.

Poem 35: I Am No Longer Who I Was

She wanted forever.
She begged for affection.
She said yes
just to feel safe.

That woman is gone.
And I do not grieve her.
I thank her for surviving.

Poem 36: Not This Time

This time,
I did not beg.
I did not explain.
I did not hold the door open
just in case.

This time,
I let it close.

Poem 37: I Am Allowed to Outgrow You

Even if we were close.
Even if we had history.
Even if I once needed you.

I am allowed
to grow in a direction
you never cared to follow.

Poem 38: I Never Forgot

The things I let slide.
The times I said,
"It's okay,"
when it wasn't.

I never forgot.
I just forgave myself
for allowing it.

Poem 39: Becoming Softer Took Strength

It was easy to harden.
To swear off hope.
To raise my voice louder than my fear.

But softness came back
like light through the cracks.
And I let it in.

Poem 40: My Life Is My Own

It no longer fits
into anyone else's plan.

I do not wait.
I do not explain.
I do not ask for permission.

This life is mine now.
And it is beautiful.

Poem 41: I Am Still Worthy

Even after mistakes.
Even after the silence.
Even after giving my heart
to the wrong hands.

I am still worthy
of softness
and safe places.

Poem 42: I Didn't Ask for Much

Just time.
Just honesty.
Just a love
that didn't make me question
myself.

That wasn't too much.
That was the bare minimum.

Poem 43: She Found Her Voice Again

It didn't return
in a scream.
It came back
as a whisper.

Steady.
Sure.
Unapologetic.

Poem 44: It Was Not My Fault

For loving him too much.
For not seeing the signs.
For believing in something
that broke me.

I didn't fail.
I just trusted
before I learned
what trust should feel like.

Poem 45: Her Boundaries Are Quiet

She doesn't yell anymore.
She doesn't explain.

She just steps away
from anything
that doesn't honour
her peace.

Poem 46: This Is What Love Feels Like Now

It's slow.
It's kind.
It doesn't make me flinch
when I hear the door.

It feels like home
with all the windows open.

Poem 47: I Am Not Tired of Feeling

Even when it hurts.
Even when it makes no sense.
Even when it's messy.

Feeling means I'm alive.
And that is not something
I want to give up.

Poem 48: The Goodbye That Saved Me

It wasn't loud.
It wasn't final.
It just needed to happen.

And once I said it,
I breathed
like I hadn't in years.

Poem 49: My Hands Are Not Empty

They carry books.
They hold warmth.
They open doors
without waiting
for someone else
to walk in first.

My hands are full of life.

Poem 50: I Kept the Light On

Even in heartbreak.
Even in fear.
Even when no one saw me.

I kept the light on.
And one day
I looked in the mirror
and realised
it had always been for me.

Poem 51: She Doesn't Chase Anymore

Not love.
Not attention.
Not the people
who only showed up
when it was easy.

She doesn't chase.
She chooses.

Poem 52: This Softness Is Earned

You do not know
how many nights
she sat alone
and still chose gentleness
over anger.

This softness
was not handed to her.
She built it
through every scar.

Poem 53: I Walked Away Without a Map

No plan.
No speech.
No closure.

I just knew
I couldn't stay
where I kept losing myself.

Poem 54: I Am Allowed to Start Again

Not because I failed.
But because I grew.

Because the life I built
stopped fitting
who I've become.

Poem 55: I Refused to Stay Small

I wore my voice quietly
for too long.
Tried to be light
so I wouldn't feel like a burden.

Now I know
the people who love you
do not need you
to be quiet.

Poem 56: She Carried the Ending Alone

He moved on.
They forgot.
But she carried the ending
like a second heart.

And when she finally let it go,
it did not hurt less.
It just hurt clean.

Poem 57: I Still Cry

But now
I cry for myself.
For how long I went unheard.
For the way I forgave
without being asked.

These tears are mine.
And they are holy.

Poem 58: I Never Needed to Be Fixed

I needed space.
I needed truth.
I needed rest.

But I never needed
to be changed
to be loved.

Poem 59: No More Begging

I do not beg
to be seen.
To be kept.
To be believed.

If they cannot see your light,
do not lower yourself
to show them.

Poem 60: I Stayed With Myself

When everyone left.
When the nights were long.
When even I
doubted my worth.

I stayed.
And that
is what saved me.

Poem 61: I Am Not Finished Yet

There is still more to write.
More to feel.
More to become.

Do not call me healed
just because I smile.
This is still a process.
And I'm still growing.

Poem 62: I Was Never Difficult

I asked for honesty.
I needed time.
I spoke when it mattered.

They called that difficult.
I call that real.

Poem 63: This Is Not the End

The silence feels final.
But I know better now.

Some endings
are just chapters
that needed a pause
so you could breathe.

Poem 64: I Choose Softness Anyway

Even when it's easier
to be cold.
Even when I've been told
to toughen up.

I choose softness
because it feels
like home in my hands.

Poem 65: They Will Talk

They will say I changed.
They will say I gave up.
They will say I walked away
too soon.

Let them talk.
They weren't the ones
losing sleep in my silence.

Poem 66: I Know Now

I know what red flags feel like
even when they are dressed
in warmth.

I know the sound
of someone slowly leaving.

And I know when to choose
my peace
instead of trying again.

Poem 67: Some Things I Will Not Carry Anymore

Their guilt.
Their silence.
The weight of not being enough
for someone who never saw me.

I leave it here.
I walk forward
lighter.

Poem 68: You Will Not Break Me

You can ignore me.
You can forget me.
You can speak of me
in unkind ways.

But you will not break me.
I already survived
what you will never understand.

Poem 69: I Am Still Becoming

Even now.
Even after all this.
Even after finding peace.

I am still learning
how to live
without fear.
And that is still
a beginning.

Poem 70: I Am the Light Now

I waited for someone
to bring me home.
To carry my sorrow.
To fix what had fallen apart.

But I was the one
who held the match.
And I lit
my own way out.

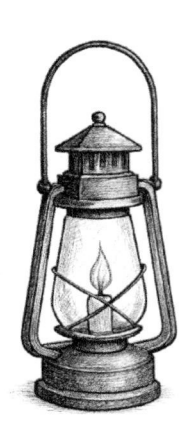

Poem 71: This Time, I Knew What to Look For

Not the butterflies.
Not the rush.
Not the attention that faded too fast.

This time,
I looked for calm.
I looked for truth.
I looked for someone
who didn't make me feel
like too much.

Poem 72: I Outgrew the Cage

It used to feel safe.
Predictable.
Mine.

But then I stretched.
And I hit the walls.
And I knew
I couldn't stay.

Poem 73: I Am Not Sorry Anymore

For asking questions.
For speaking up.
For saying no
without guilt tied to it.

I am not sorry
for becoming a woman
who chooses herself.

Poem 74: The Quiet Kept Me Safe

It held me
when nothing else did.
When noise only made things worse.

The quiet became
a place where I could hear
my own heart
without interruption.

Poem 75: I Carried Myself Home

No hand to hold.
No map.
No one waiting on the porch.

Just me.
And the knowing
that I was worth coming back for.

Step by step,
I carried myself home.

A Final Note

You made it.
Not just to the end of this book,
but through every hard thing
that brought you here.

If these poems reminded you
of your strength,
your softness,
your voice,
then this book has done
what it came to do.

You do not need to be perfect.
You only need to be real.
You only need to be *you*.

Keep choosing yourself.
Again and again.

With love,
Isobel Raine

Printed in Dunstable, United Kingdom